miley cyrus

YEARBOOK 2009

We are family

Boy, was 1992 a fantastic year for Billy Ray Cyrus! Not only was his number one single 'Achy Breaky Heart' topping the charts all over the globe, but his superstar daughter came into the world. On November 23, Destiny Hope Cyrus – Miley's birth name – was born. Her proud mullet-wielding daddy took one look into her ocean-blue eyes and knew instantly that he was holding a future star in his arms.

Just like the zany Stewarts in *Hannah Montana*, the Cyrus family travelled on the road together as Billy Ray toured the world with his chart-topping country tunes. Little Destiny was having such a fun and happy time touring with her father that she never stopped smiling, even as a teething toddler. Her ever-present flashing smile soon earned her the nickname 'Smiley'. After some years this was shortened to 'Miley', the name she's used ever since. In 2008, Miley made it official and legally changed her name from Destiny to Miley, using Ray as her new middle name as a testament to her dad – how sweet! Only

Miley spends rainy afternoons watching soppy chick-flicks with her sister.

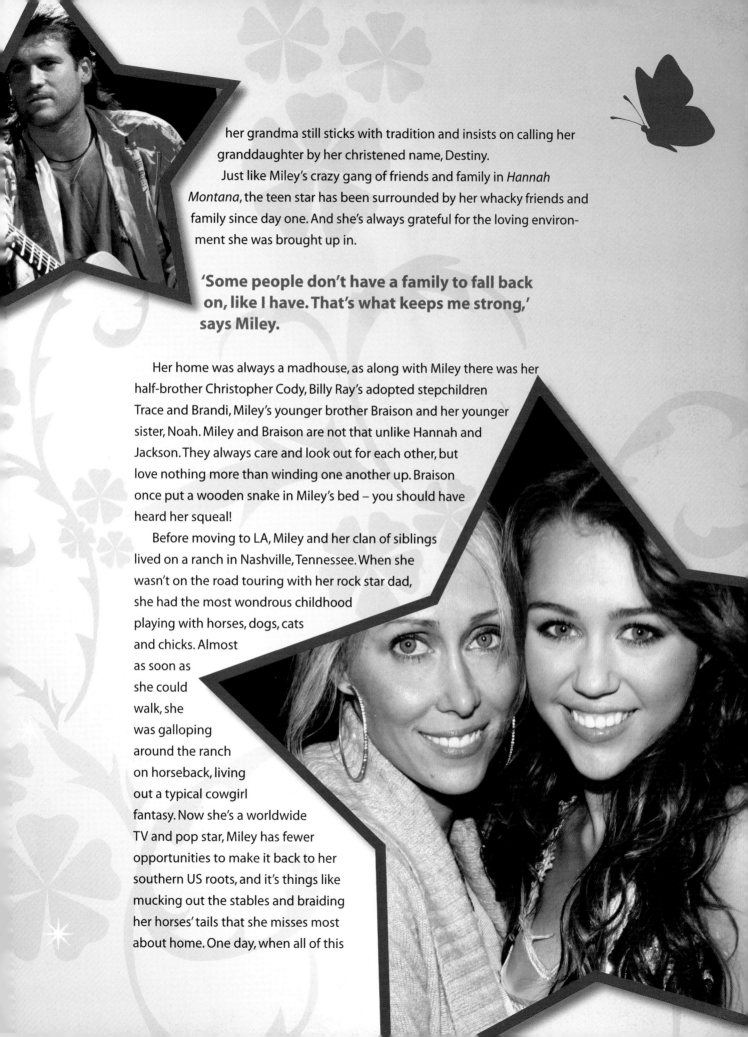

her grandma still sticks with tradition and insists on calling her granddaughter by her christened name, Destiny.

Just like Miley's crazy gang of friends and family in *Hannah Montana*, the teen star has been surrounded by her whacky friends and family since day one. And she's always grateful for the loving environment she was brought up in.

'Some people don't have a family to fall back on, like I have. That's what keeps me strong,' says Miley.

Her home was always a madhouse, as along with Miley there was her half-brother Christopher Cody, Billy Ray's adopted stepchildren Trace and Brandi, Miley's younger brother Braison and her younger sister, Noah. Miley and Braison are not that unlike Hannah and Jackson. They always care and look out for each other, but love nothing more than winding one another up. Braison once put a wooden snake in Miley's bed – you should have heard her squeal!

Before moving to LA, Miley and her clan of siblings lived on a ranch in Nashville, Tennessee. When she wasn't on the road touring with her rock star dad, she had the most wondrous childhood playing with horses, dogs, cats and chicks. Almost as soon as she could walk, she was galloping around the ranch on horseback, living out a typical cowgirl fantasy. Now she's a worldwide TV and pop star, Miley has fewer opportunities to make it back to her southern US roots, and it's things like mucking out the stables and braiding her horses' tails that she misses most about home. One day, when all of this

Hollywood mania is over, she'd love nothing more than to set up a big old ranch, just like the one she grew up on, and having herself weekly hoedowns and the like. Yee haw, cowgirl!

A YOUNG STAR ...

With a rockin' and rollin' father like Billy Ray, not to mention having Dolly Parton – the queen of country and western – as her godmother, it was inevitable that Miley would be singing as soon as she was able to crawl.

'My dad says I could sing before I could talk, if that's possible. I was always humming and things like that,' says Miley.

At the teeny age of only two, she was already warming up for her role of playing superstar Hannah Montana, as she would waddle on stage to sing with her dad:

'I would sing "Hound Dog" and silly songs for the fun of it.'

Her superstar qualities were there for all to see from a very young age. She was forever parading around the house in front of people and she revelled in attention: 'When I was little, I would stand up on couches and exclaim, "Watch me!" We had these showers that are completely glass, and I would lock people in them and make them stay in there and watch me perform.' Wow, can you imagine watching a private performance from Hannah Montana? You should be so lucky!

So from day one, Miley was following her destiny to sing and dance. But she didn't always receive applause for her performances. Remember the *Hannah Montana* episode where Miley was forced to be a pirate, her school's mascot, instead of a cheerleader? Well, she knows all about embarrassing herself in front of her school pals. When trying out for her school dance team, she fell over and ripped her denim skirt in front of all the boys while practising in the school hallway. Needless to say, her face was as red as a ripe tomato with embarrassment!

AUDITION LIMBO

In 2005, the executives at Disney were considering the idea of making a show based on a *That's So Raven* episode in which a child star of a popular TV show attends a local school and tries to lead a normal life. Initially, they couldn't decide on a name – Anna Cabana, Samantha York and Alexis Texas were all possibilities.

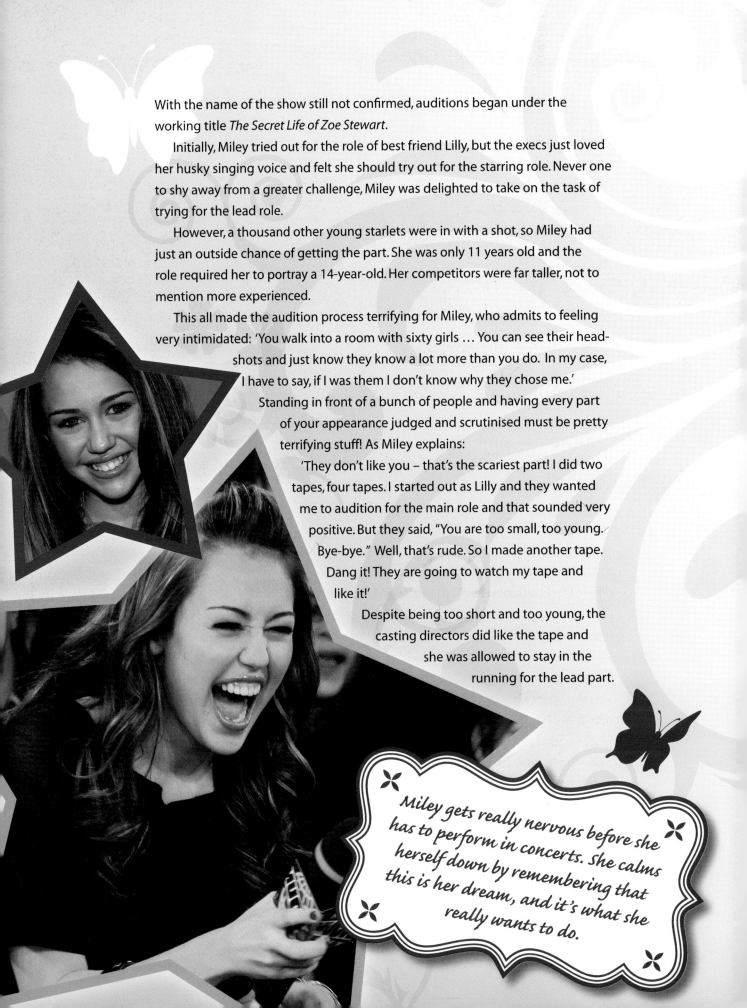

With the name of the show still not confirmed, auditions began under the working title *The Secret Life of Zoe Stewart*.

Initially, Miley tried out for the role of best friend Lilly, but the execs just loved her husky singing voice and felt she should try out for the starring role. Never one to shy away from a greater challenge, Miley was delighted to take on the task of trying for the lead role.

However, a thousand other young starlets were in with a shot, so Miley had just an outside chance of getting the part. She was only 11 years old and the role required her to portray a 14-year-old. Her competitors were far taller, not to mention more experienced.

This all made the audition process terrifying for Miley, who admits to feeling very intimidated: 'You walk into a room with sixty girls … You can see their head-shots and just know they know a lot more than you do. In my case, I have to say, if I was them I don't know why they chose me.'

Standing in front of a bunch of people and having every part of your appearance judged and scrutinised must be pretty terrifying stuff! As Miley explains:

'They don't like you – that's the scariest part! I did two tapes, four tapes. I started out as Lilly and they wanted me to audition for the main role and that sounded very positive. But they said, "You are too small, too young. Bye-bye." Well, that's rude. So I made another tape. Dang it! They are going to watch my tape and like it!'

Despite being too short and too young, the casting directors did like the tape and she was allowed to stay in the running for the lead part.

Miley gets really nervous before she has to perform in concerts. She calms herself down by remembering that this is her dream, and it's what she really wants to do.

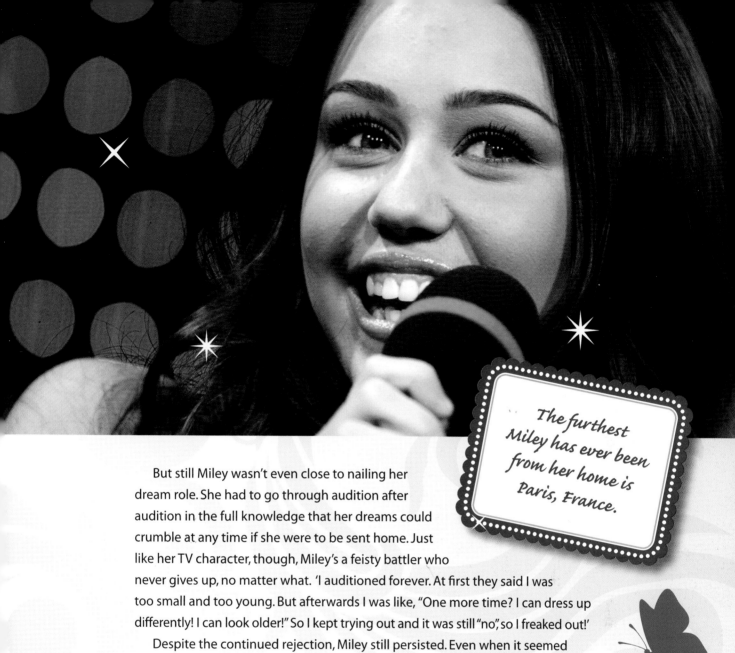

But still Miley wasn't even close to nailing her dream role. She had to go through audition after audition in the full knowledge that her dreams could crumble at any time if she were to be sent home. Just like her TV character, though, Miley's a feisty battler who never gives up, no matter what. 'I auditioned forever. At first they said I was too small and too young. But afterwards I was like, "One more time? I can dress up differently! I can look older!" So I kept trying out and it was still "no", so I freaked out!'

Despite the continued rejection, Miley still persisted. Even when it seemed that everything was against her, and disaster struck on one of her final auditions, she still stuck at it. 'I had lost my teeth before the audition, my front teeth, four of them had braces on top. Even though I talk a lot, my mouth and face is tiny. I was sitting there with huge buckteeth and huge braces and huge hair and a tiny little body. But four months later the producers were like "Come to California".' So braces and all, when it came to star quality, none of the other hopefuls could hold a torch to Miley's beaming radiance.

With this exciting news, Miley packed her bags and, like so many other wannabes, headed for Hollywood. 'We went out [to California] and I auditioned one more time, and I got the part,' she says. Miley proved to herself and everyone else that determination, guts and having a dream are all you need to make it in Hollywood. Oh, and it helps if you can sing, dance and act a little as well!

The Miley Quiz

Think you know everything there is to know about the honky tonk heroine? Take the Miley quiz and see how many points you score to see if you're her biggest know-it-all fan.

1 What is Miley's original name?
- a) Maggie May Cyrus
- b) Miley Ray Cyrus
- c) Jeanie Ray Cyrus
- ✓ d) Destiny Hope Cyrus

2 What is Miley's star sign?
- ✓ a) Sagittarius
- b) Aries
- c) Libra
- d) Scorpio

3 Where is Miley's hometown?
- a) Malibu
- ✓ b) Nashville
- c) Houston
- d) Dallas

d ✗ **4 Who is Miley's favourite actor?**
- ✓ a) Johnny Depp
- b) Brad Pitt
- c) Jack Black
- d) Orlando Bloom

d ✗ **5 Apart from her dad, of course, who is her favourite musician?**
- ✓ a) Christina Aguilera
- b) Joss Stone
- c) Amy Winehouse
- d) Hilary Duff

6 What nickname has Miley's family been calling her since she was a baby?
- a) Buttons
- ✓ b) Smiley
- c) Whiney
- d) Dolly

7 What is Miley's favourite animal?
- a) Cat
- b) Tiger
- c) Hippo
- ✓ d) Dog

8 What is Miley's top movie?
- a) *Goonies*
- ✓ b) *Steel Magnolias*
- c) *Shrek*
- d) *High School Musical*

✗ **9 Who is Miley's all-time number one author?**
- *b* ✓ a) JK Rowling
- b) Roald Dahl
- c) JRR Tolkein
- d) CS Lewis

10 *What gives Miley the creeps more than anything?*
- a) Spiders
- ✓ b) Snakes
- c) Worms
- d) Birds

a ✗

11 *When Miley turns into Hannah Montana, what favourite snack does she like having in her dressing room?*
- a) Cheeseburgers
- b) Hot dogs
- c) Fries
- ✓ d) Sandwiches

b ✗

12 *What is Miley's all-time favourite TV show?*
- ✓ a) *Gossip Girl*
- b) *The O.C.*
- c) *Laguna Beach*
- d) *Summerland*

d ✗

13 *What is Miley's worst habit?*
- a) Biting her nails
- b) Picking her nose
- c) Humming
- ✓ d) Talking with a full mouth

a ✗

14 *What was Miley's dad, Billy Ray's, biggest hit single?*
- a) Ice Ice Baby
- b) It Won't Be The Last
- ✓ c) Achy Breaky Heart
- d) Hammer Time

15 *Who is Miley's favourite Hollywood actress?*
- a) Angelina Jolie
- ✓ b) Jennifer Aniston
- c) Julia Roberts
- d) Natalie Portman

16 *What is Miley's younger sister's name?*
- a) Angie May
- b) Nora Sue
- c) Jeanie Jane
- ✓ d) Noah Lindsey

17 *What smell does Miley like to have all around her house?*
- a) Roses
- ✓ b) Vanilla
- c) Chocolate
- d) Cheese

18 *Which celebrity does Miley have a HUGE crush on?*
- a) Chad Michael Murray
- b) Zac Efron
- c) Justin Timberlake
- ✓ d) Colin Farrell

a ✗

19 *Which musical icon did Miley cover the first time she sang on stage?*
- a) Elvis
- b) Johnny Cash
- ✓ c) Madonna
- d) Kylie Minogue

a ✗

20 *Who is Miley's celebrity godmother?*
- a) Cher
- b) Madonna
- ✓ c) Dolly Parton
- d) Joan Collins

How many did you score? Add up your points to see how much of a Miley know-it-all you are. Answers on page 61

16–20 You know more about Miley than she knows about herself – you're her number one Hannahtastic fan!

11–15 Wow! You really know your stuff – you're a top fan.

6–10 You know your Miley facts, but not enough – you're a could-do-better fan.

0–5 You need to get studying up on your Miley knowledge – you're a half-hearted Hannah fan.

Test your friends and see who knows Hannah the best.

Hannah Montana arrives

 n 24 March 2006, *Hannah Montana* was aired on the Disney Channel for the very first time. The show pulled in a record audience of 5.4 million viewers and, needless to say, they absolutely loved it. Kids across America fell in love with Hannah, Miley and her whacky gang of close friends and family. In no time the show went global, reaching an astonishing 164 million viewers worldwide. Almost overnight, little Miley Ray Cyrus had gone from a small-time farm girl to international superstar.

Miley says that she looks up to former Disney teen queen Hilary Duff for staying true to herself and not being fake.

Working alongside her dad, the show is semi-autobiographical and the close relationship between Miley and Billy Ray is evident for all to see. She really is the luckiest girl in the world. Not only is she a worldwide superstar in her own right, but she gets to work with her loving megastar daddy, too!

What so many folk love about the show is getting to see both sides of Miley Ray Cyrus. For so many stars, we only get to see their performing persona, but while we get plenty of that when Miley is Hannah, we also get to see what her family life must be like when she plays home bird Miley Ray Stewart.

MORE SUCCESS!

The first season was so well loved by all, Disney had to extend it by a further four episodes. When the second season was aired, the praise kept coming in and it was clear that the world had officially gone crazy for *Hannah Montana*.

'Outstanding Female Lead in a Comedy Series (Child or Adolescent)' at the 2008 Gracie Allen Awards

'Choice TV Actress in a Comedy' at the 2007 Teen Choice Awards

'Choice Summer Artist' at the 2007 Teen Choice Awards

'Favourite TV Actress' at the 2007 Kids' Choice Awards

'Favourite TV Actress' at the 2008 Kids' Choice Awards

'Favourite Female Singer' at the 2008 Kids' Choice Awards

So, the logical progression was to take the *Hannah Montana* show on tour. That way, everyone could see Miley perform all of Hannah's songs live. Once she's on stage, Miley really shows the audience why she's such a huge star and blows them away with her fantastically husky voice and spectacular dance routines. Despite it being really hard work, Miley realises it's all worth it when she's in front of the crowd:

'Looking at the crowd, seeing their faces and hearing them say the positive words of the songs is really important for me.'

In no time, Miley has transformed Hannah Montana into an overnight star, and just like the TV show, having an alternate personality allows her to lead a normal life at home. Only unlike the show, everybody is in on the secret that beneath the blonde wig it's really Miley Cyrus. No doubt in time she'll soon grow out of being Hannah and will start to release music under her real name. But for the time being she's happy being Hannah and Miley. Who wouldn't be? She really does get the best of both worlds!

Make Your Own
MILEY BADGE

Show off to your friends that you are Miley's biggest fan with your very own homemade Miley badges.

You will need:

Lots of different pictures of Miley or Hannah cut out from magazines

Old badges

Scissors

Glue

Coloured pens

Instructions:

1 Choose a badge that's a similar size to Miley's face in one of your pictures.

2 Place the badge over the picture of Miley's face and use your scissors to cut out the picture of Miley around the badge.

3 Using your glue, stick the picture of Miley to the badge.

4 With a colourful pen write things like 'HANNAH ROCKS', or your name and Miley's on the badge.

5 If you want, you could stick your picture on the badge next to Miley's face, or use glitter pens to add that extra sparkle.

Design Your
PERFECT POP STAR

Reckon you could rock out the show more than Miss Montana? Well, first you've got to get the look, and we can show you how …

Instructions:

1 *Look at lots of magazines to see what your favourite pop stars are wearing at the moment. If you want your pop star to look like Hannah, you should design her trademark bright, rock-chick clothing. Or you could try something different. What about cool ripped jeans and a black T-shirt with funky accessories for an emo pop star? Or you could do the hoedown in style with a country and western look like Miley's godmother, Dolly Parton.*

2 *Once you've chosen your look, cut out the clothes from the pieces of paper and colour them. Using your glue, stick them to the different Miley and Hannah mannequins.*

3 *Now you should decide on the hair and make-up. Use your coloured pens to add make-up to the face and to draw your hair-style. Do you want to go blonde or brunette, long or short? What style of make-up would you prefer – glittery, grungey or natural? What about blusher and lipstick?*

4 Using the tinfoil, cut out any accessories you'd like, such as necklaces or rings. Think about what your favourite pop stars, like Hannah, wear. She normally goes for sparkly earrings, a simple necklace and a pretty bracelet.

What songs would you sing at your first gig? Write down your playlist here.

goodbye, just a girl, supergirl, he could be the one, don't wannabe turn, best of both worlds

Hannah Montana

Miley is the luckiest girl in the world as she gets to combine being a film, TV and pop star all in one character. 'I've always loved singing, and I've always loved acting and dancing,' says Miley. 'Getting this opportunity with Disney, I get to do it all. They let you do everything you love.'

'It all starts from the root of it, which is the show. And that's showing a normal girl who also has a huge dream and she's getting to live it … and everyone has that. I think no matter whether it's for singing or acting or whatever you want to do, everyone has that dream that they want to go for,' says Miley. And that's why we love her. Miley and Hannah are total role models – they represent both the reality and the dream – the dream we all have to be famous and be a pop star.

HANNAH MONTANA SEASON ONE

When we first meet a young Miley Stewart in Episode One, she's struggling to keep her double identity a secret. She soon realises that when it comes to close friends, honesty is the best policy, so she lets Lilly in on her big secret.

Once she lets her BFFs, Oliver and Lilly, in on her secret, she doesn't have to sneak around so much. For Lilly – or Lola as she becomes known when with Hannah – it does take some getting used to, as she gets a little star-struck at all the celebrity bashes and loses her cool. Hannah certainly learns the lesson that friendship is more important than all the cool perks you get as a celebrity.

Throughout the series we are also introduced to various characters

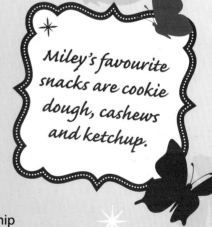

Miley's favourite snacks are cookie dough, cashews and ketchup.

18

and 'frenemies' such as Amber, Ashley and Rico, who have various confrontations with Miley, Lilly, Oliver and Jackson.

Without a doubt, the highlight of the first season is the introduction of Jake Ryan, a celebrity and hunk who joins Miley's class at Seaview Middle School. Of course, everyone goes crazy for him, but he only has eyes for our Miley. Miley, of course, is not impressed by his star status and claims to loathe him. But she soon gives in to his gorgeous charms and eventually they kiss, only for him to go off to shoot a film, leaving Miley in the lurch. Poor Miley, what a disaster!

Hannah also gets to meet the Queen and does a special bonus episode with the *That's So Raven* gang and Zack and Cody. But which is your favourite show from Season One?

MILEY'S TOP 5 EPISODES IN SEASON ONE

Episode 18
'People Who Use People'
Obviously, this is a favourite of everyone. Miley's first on-screen kiss with Jake is a huge moment, but it's all so sad when we hear that Jake has to go to Romania for four months.

Episode 16
'Good Golly Miss Dolly'
After suffering a little boy trouble, Miley's off-screen godmother, Dolly Parton, comes into town to help her out. Dolly also gives a feminine touch to the Stewart household, much to the detriment of Jackson and Robbie's volumised hair!

(cont.)

Episode 15
'More Than a Zombie To Me'

Again this one's a special episode for Miley because she plays opposite the hunk, Jake Ryan. Of course, Miley doesn't quite realise her feelings for the superstar and blows him out when he invites her to the school dance. But it all gets a bit weird when he ends up going with Lilly of all people.

Episode 12
'On the Road Again'

Guest starring Ashley Tisdale, one of Miley's off-screen best friends, this episode is scarily accurate to Miley's actual life. Robbie Ray tries his hand in the music business and jets off to play a live gig. He soon realises that despite how much he loves playing music, being with his family is far more important.

Episode 7
'It's a Mannequin's World'

With Miley's birthday coming up, Robbie Ray goes shopping for her birthday present. As per usual, his taste leaves something to be desired and he buys something that would be more suitable for a six-year-old. It turns out that Robbie can't help but think of his teenage daughter as a little girl – another episode that's not too far from reality, eh, Billy Ray?

HANNAH MONTANA SEASON TWO

The second season sees an older Miley start high school, and with greater responsibilities and a more mature environment, Miley learns to balance her school and showbiz life. Of course, a major junction in this season is the return of Miley's major love interest, Jake Ryan.

Again, Miley has to go through the dilemma of deciding whether to reveal her secret identity to another person. But can anyone really get close to Miley without knowing her great secret?

Meanwhile along with great loves come great enemies. Hannah finds an annoying rival in the form of Mikayla. Plus Jackson's boss, Rico, becomes more of a permanent feature in the show and, of course, makes a nuisance of himself at every opportunity.

With *Hannah Montana* now established as television's number one show, more guest stars arrive including the Jonas Brothers and Jesse McCartney. Happily for Miley, they're all real hotties – lucky girl!

MILEY'S TOP 5 EPISODES IN SEASON TWO

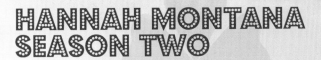

Episode 9 and 10 'Achy Jakey Heart'

This double episode features the return of the gorgeous babe Jake Ryan. Initially, Miley isn't too impressed with the star, but after a while she succumbs to his charms. So, after much deliberation, she lets him in on her secret, only to realise that the superstar heart-throb finds it hard to function in a normal environment. But if Miley wanted a superstar lifestyle all the time, she'd tell everyone she was Hannah. In the end, she has no choice but to dump the hunk.

(cont.) 21

MILEY'S TOP 5 EPISODES IN SEASON TWO

Episode 12
'When You Wish You Were the Star'

This is a classic episode in which Miley wishes she could always be Hannah. Well, be careful what you wish for! Despite dating super babe Jesse McCartney – hubba hubba! – Miley realises that being an international celeb 24/7 isn't all it's cracked up to be.

Episode 16
'Me and Mr. Jonas and Mr. Jonas and Mr. Jonas'

Wonder why Miley loves this episode so much? Nothing to do with a giant crush on Nick Jonas, who stars in it, perhaps? Miley gets jealous when her dad writes songs with Kevin, Joe and Nick of the Jonas Brothers. However, in the end, lucky Hannah gets to sing with the trio.

Episode 18
'That's What Friends Are For'

Jake Ryan comes back into town again and, having assured Miley that her secret is safe despite their break-up, he tells Miley they should just be friends. Miley isn't so sure and her doubts are increased when she finds out that Hannah's arch rival, Mikayla, has been cast opposite her former beau.

Episode 28 'Yet Another Side of Me'

Having been influenced by an older musician, Miley decides it's time to change Hannah's image ... to a rock chick! Unfortunately, but unsurprisingly, the look doesn't go down so well and Miley learns a valuable lesson – stick to what you do best and don't be so easily influenced in the future.

HANNAH OR MILEY?

Playing two amazing roles in the same show must be a lot of fun, but which of the two characters is most like Miley Cyrus? 'I relate more to the Miley character because that's kind of how I am when I'm not working. We go and get ice cream down the street. I like my Miley Stewart life, and when I go to the set I definitely feel like I'm living the script.'

She certainly is living the script, getting to hang out with her friends and family, having a 'normal' life by day and rocking the show by night.

Do you feel like chilling out and taking it slow, or do you want to rock out the show? Take the personality quiz to find if you are a mellow Miley or a hard-rock Hannah ...

Are you having a MILEY day or a HANNAH day?

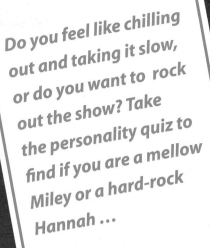

1 *When you wake up in the morning and are setting off for school, are you ...*
- a) Exhausted from rockin' out last night
- ✓ b) Fresh and excited about seeing your friends

2 *How do you like to wear your hair?*
- ✓ a) Blonde and straight
- b) Brunette and wavy

3 *Friday nights are all about ...*
- ✓ a) Partying, baby!
- b) Hanging out with family and ordering in pizza

4 *Saturday afternoons are for ...*
- a) Work, work, work!
- ✓ b) Hitting the beach with your pals

5 *Your ideal day at home is spent ...*
- ✓ a) Doing singing practice
- b) Goofing around with your brother

6 Your wardrobe is …
- a) Big enough to throw a party in
- ✓ b) Small but tasteful and elegant

7 At school you …
- a) Get mobbed by everyone wanting to be your pal
- ✓ b) Hang out with your real friends

8 At the mall you …
- a) Can never get any shopping done because of the crowds that follow you
- ✓ b) Spend all the time you like choosing your clothes

9 What do you think of make-up?
- ✓ a) Plenty of it please, but keep it classy
- b) Just a touch – I like the natural look

10 What do you think of being in front of an audience?
- ✓ a) You love the attention and adoration
- b) You'd rather be in the crowd than in front of it

So how did you get on? Find out by counting up which letter you answered the most.

How did you get on? If you scored mostly …

A's then you're a Hannah Montana-a-like. You just can't get enough of being a star, can you girl? You love the glitz and glamour of Hollywood. But just be wary because the spotlight might leave no room for privacy in your life.

B's then you're a Miley Ray girl. You're a home bird who just loves to be with her friends and family, and never craves adoration. Remember that a little attention in your life isn't always a bad thing.

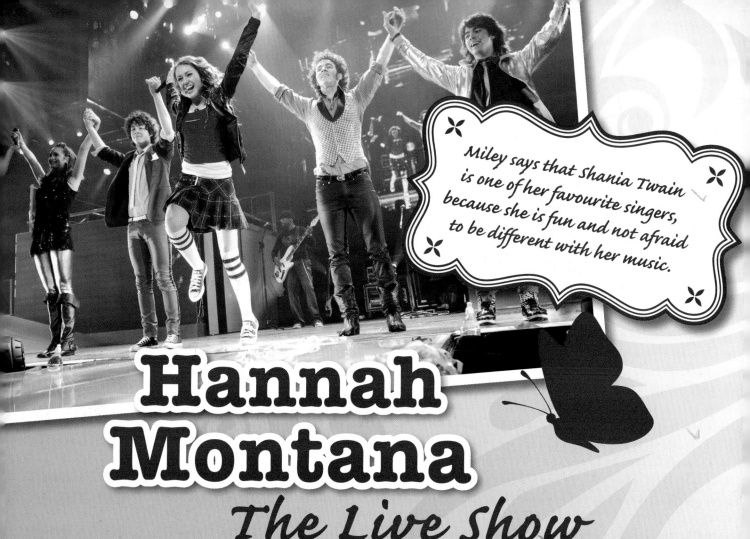

Hannah Montana
The Live Show

It makes perfect sense that Miley would want to bring the on-screen pop star to the stage. And with millions of fans worldwide, she knew she'd easily sell out any stadium. So Miley packed her bags – just like her honky tonk dad more than a decade earlier – and brought her show to the world.

The training was pretty intense. There's quite a big difference between doing a weekly TV programme and strutting your stuff in front of thousands of screaming fans, but Miley was able to handle the transition ... just.

'We finished shooting the last episode of *Hannah Montana* and then the very next day I woke up at nine a.m, started running with a trainer and had to get into rehearsals. It's been great, though, I feel so good, not just physically from being fit and being on tour, but also mentally.'

Once Miley was physically ready for the live show, there was nothing left to do but jump on the tour bus and hit the road. But someone was missing – her ever-present daddy had to stay behind.

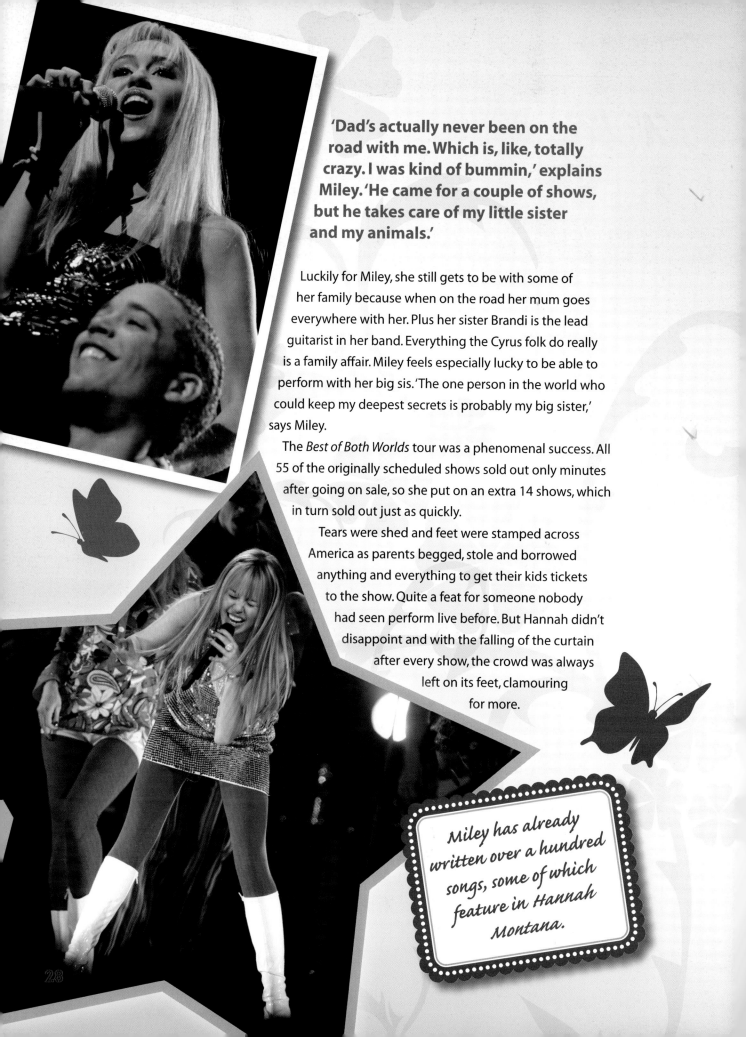

'Dad's actually never been on the road with me. Which is, like, totally crazy. I was kind of bummin,' explains Miley. 'He came for a couple of shows, but he takes care of my little sister and my animals.'

Luckily for Miley, she still gets to be with some of her family because when on the road her mum goes everywhere with her. Plus her sister Brandi is the lead guitarist in her band. Everything the Cyrus folk do really is a family affair. Miley feels especially lucky to be able to perform with her big sis. 'The one person in the world who could keep my deepest secrets is probably my big sister,' says Miley.

The *Best of Both Worlds* tour was a phenomenal success. All 55 of the originally scheduled shows sold out only minutes after going on sale, so she put on an extra 14 shows, which in turn sold out just as quickly.

Tears were shed and feet were stamped across America as parents begged, stole and borrowed anything and everything to get their kids tickets to the show. Quite a feat for someone nobody had seen perform live before. But Hannah didn't disappoint and with the falling of the curtain after every show, the crowd was always left on its feet, clamouring for more.

Miley has already written over a hundred songs, some of which feature in Hannah Montana.

Miley WORDSEARCH

Search for the words listed below in the grid. The words can run horizontally, diagonally or from top to bottom.

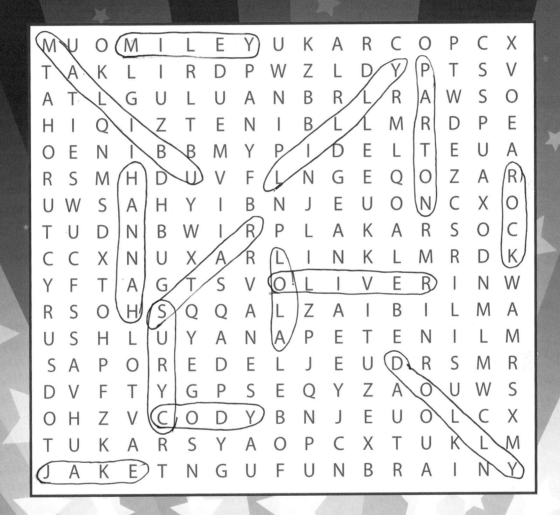

Hidden words:

- MILEY
- HANNAH
- MALIBU
- PARTON
- JAKE
- OLIVER
- ROCK
- CYRUS
- DOLLY
- CODY
- LOLA
- LILLY
- STAR

Steal Miley's Style

No matter where she's going or what she's doing, Miley is always the most gorgeous and trendy girl in the room. Whether she's glamming it up for the Oscars or nipping out for sushi with her pals, being a teen icon means she has to look her best at all times – you never know when those pesky paparazzi are going to pop out of the bushes. Listen in as Miley gives away her top-secret fashion tips ...

DRESSING UP

'If I have the opportunity to get dressed up then I like to be bold, out-there, crazy and fun. When I went to the Oscars, I felt like Cinderella for the night. I loved it. Valentino designed my dress, which was so thrilling for me. It was his very last collection because he's declared his retirement from fashion now, so my design was the last design he ever made. How cool is that?'

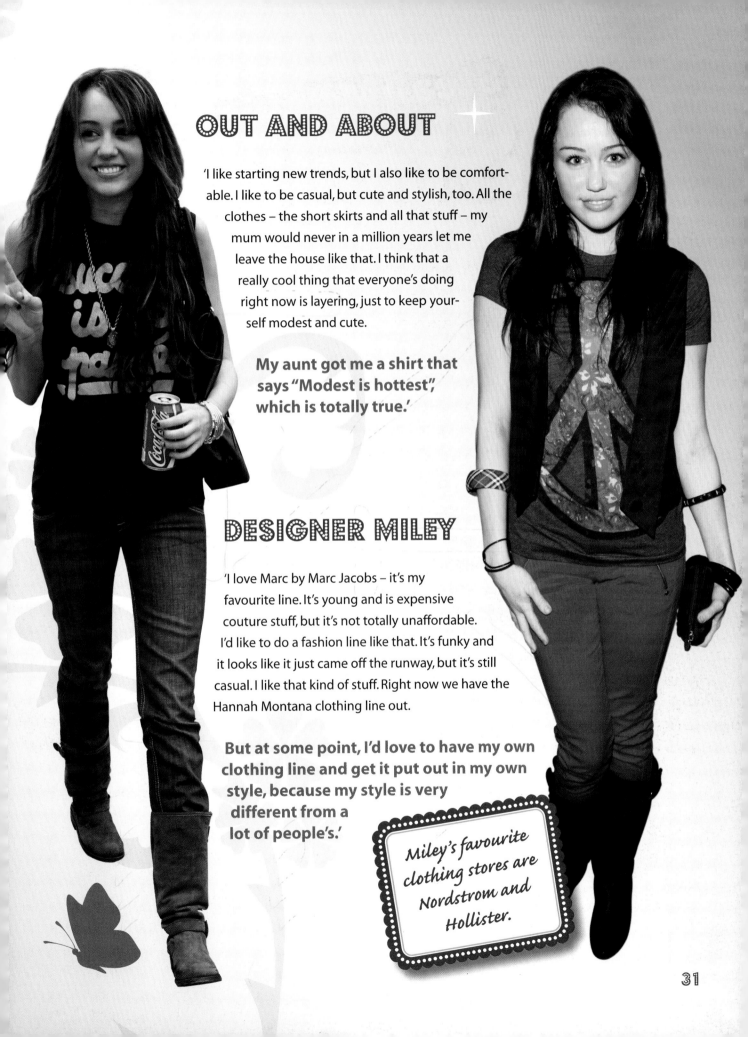

OUT AND ABOUT

'I like starting new trends, but I also like to be comfortable. I like to be casual, but cute and stylish, too. All the clothes – the short skirts and all that stuff – my mum would never in a million years let me leave the house like that. I think that a really cool thing that everyone's doing right now is layering, just to keep yourself modest and cute.

My aunt got me a shirt that says "Modest is hottest", which is totally true.'

DESIGNER MILEY

'I love Marc by Marc Jacobs – it's my favourite line. It's young and is expensive couture stuff, but it's not totally unaffordable. I'd like to do a fashion line like that. It's funky and it looks like it just came off the runway, but it's still casual. I like that kind of stuff. Right now we have the Hannah Montana clothing line out.

But at some point, I'd love to have my own clothing line and get it put out in my own style, because my style is very different from a lot of people's.'

Miley's favourite clothing stores are Nordstrom and Hollister.

CHOOSING YOUR STYLE

'I always say that confidence is the greatest thing, so whatever you feel comfortable in is good.

I love wearing sweatpants. I feel really comfortable and good in them. It doesn't matter if you're not into the style that everyone else is used to – if it's a little more rock and roll or a little more preppy. If you feel comfortable, then wear it.'

MILEY AS HANNAH

'Playing Hannah is a total girl thing. It's like dressing up every day. I love all the good clothes and the shoes, and someone dressing you and having your hair and make-up done. I definitely like the glamorous part of my job, because once my face gets washed off, I'm like, "Dang it. Dang it, why can't the glamour always be around?"'

Miley had to have braces on her teeth, but the dentist was able to hide them by putting them on the other side of her teeth so no one noticed.

32

MILEY'S MAKE-UP AND SKINCARE TIPS

'I'm a big skin freak. I do my exfoliation at night and keep everything in check.

I like to take care of my body, so make sure you take care of your skin while you're young. Then it will carry on with you. I think natural-looking make-up is the best. I like to wear make-up that's as natural as can be. It's too over the top when you start caking it on.'

Miley's Make-up Masterclass

It's tough being one of the hottest teen stars in Hollywood, especially when you have to look as good popping down to the local store as you do being papped at a red-carpet award ceremony. But Miley manages to pull it off, always looking fresh and glamorous. So how does she do it and how can we get her look?

Here, you can learn some hot trade secrets and test out Miley's make-up tips, so you'll be ready for that hot party of the week!

What you'll need in your Miley/Hannah make-up bag:

Eye shadows – natural browns, golds, creams and light pinks for Miley; purples, greens and yellows for Hannah

Black eyeliner – liquid or kohl pencil

Mascara – brown or black

Blusher – pink or peach

Lip gloss – pinks and reds

Shimmer dust for cheeks

Make-up brushes

MILEY'S MAKE-UP

Miley has often said that she prefers the natural look as far as her make-up is concerned. With pink tones and plenty of lip gloss, she uses a little concealer to hide any blemishes, lots of pink blusher, smoky eye shadow and black mascara. Before you try this on your own skin, do what the stars do and, using the face below, work out exactly where all the important colours should go. Have a mirror to hand and copy your hair and eyebrow shape onto the face. Then, matching your make-up colours with either a crayon or a felt-tip pen, try out different colours on the eyelids, cheeks and lips to see what looks rockin'. It's as simple as that!

TOP TIP

Use a rosy pink blusher for light skin or a deeper pink for darker skin. When applying, use long, sweeping brush strokes starting from the apples of your cheeks (find these by giving yourself a big smile in the mirror, they are the round bits) then work back towards your ears. Add a touch to your temples and neck – just a touch, though! – to give you a sun-kissed, Hollywood look.

To get the look

Look in the mirror and hide any blemishes with a concealer that matches your skin tone – you can also smooth a little onto the upper eyelid to create an even surface upon which to apply your eye shadow.

1 For Miley eyes, first use a light brown colour and sweep all over the eyelid with a small make-up brush.

2 Then use a lighter gold in the crease of your eye or in the inner or outer corners of your lids – you can decide what looks best.

3 Blend the colours with your fingertips to create an even covering. Next, apply eyeliner to your upper eyelid – to really glam it up, add a touch to the lower lid too.

4 Then add mascara to your top and bottom lashes, starting at the base of your eyelashes and wiggling the brush from side to side as you coat the length of your lashes. If you have very long eyelashes, you may not need to use mascara. Lucky you!

Finish off your polished teen star look by adding a salmon pink lip gloss to your upper and lower lips. Blot if necessary, then reapply.

Wow! Now you are ready to meet your public. Make sure you pop a lip gloss in your handbag too – Miley never leaves the house without hers.

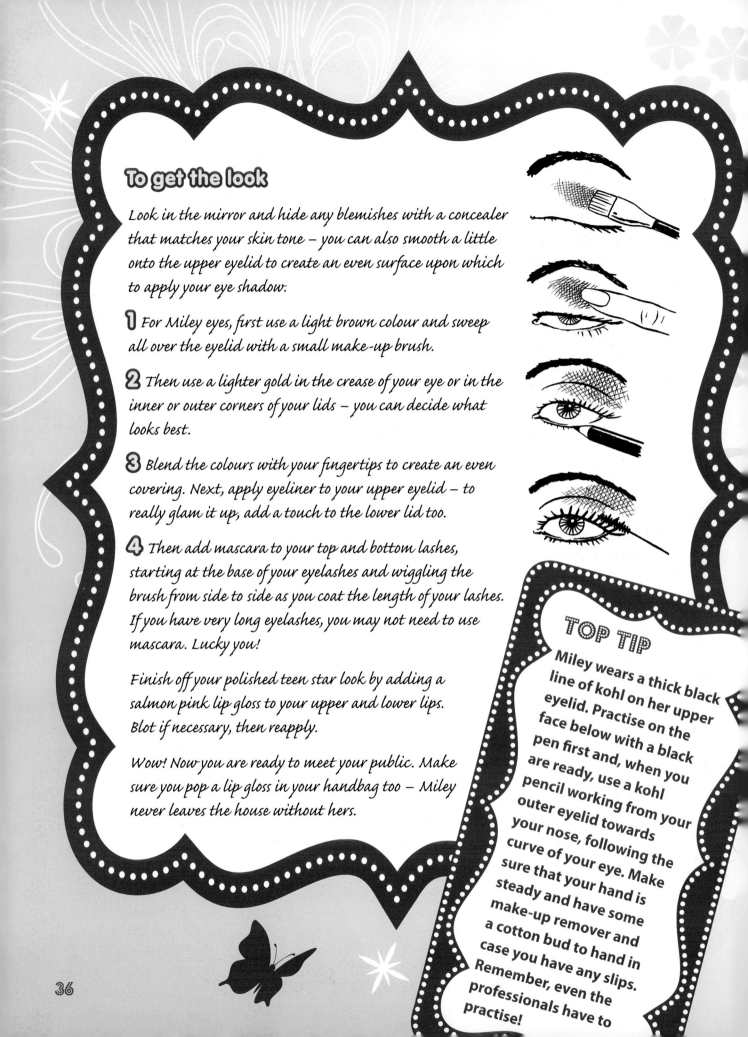

TOP TIP

Miley wears a thick black line of kohl on her upper eyelid. Practise on the face below with a black pen first and, when you are ready, use a kohl pencil working from your outer eyelid towards your nose, following the curve of your eye. Make sure that your hand is steady and have some make-up remover and a cotton bud to hand in case you have any slips. Remember, even the professionals have to practise!

HANNAH GLAM

When Miley puts on her blonde wig, the colours really come out of the make-up bag. So, this is your chance to have some fun trying out bolder shades of eye shadows and lip glosses. How about trying a rainbow of colours across your eyelid, or adding just a touch of green and purple to the corners of your eyes? Experiment using your coloured pens on the face here.

To get the look

Apply eye shadow, eyeliner, blusher and lip gloss as before, but this time really rock up the colours. Try purples, greens, stronger pinks and yellows on your eyelids and red lip gloss to pout like a pop star. Finish off the whole look by dipping your blusher brush into some shimmer dust and lightly add to your cheeks and temples. You can even add a touch of sparkle to your hair and clothes too. For Hannah, there's no such thing as overdoing the bling!

TOP TIP

Before applying the brighter colours of Hannah's make-up, make sure you moisturise your skin. That way any mistakes you make or colours you don't like can easily be removed with a facial wipe or cotton wool and make-up remover.

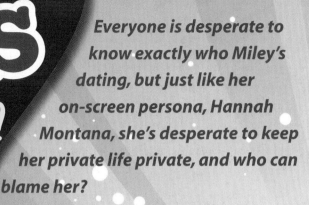

BOYS SAY WHAT?

Everyone is desperate to know exactly who Miley's dating, but just like her on-screen persona, Hannah Montana, she's desperate to keep her private life private, and who can blame her?

Still, everyone's speculating about her love life, and we're all desperate to know which lucky guy holds her heart. No one according to Miley: 'I think I'm too much to handle right now. There's so much going on in my life at the moment with travelling, and there's always cameras following me – all that kind of stuff. I don't think it's great for dating anyone. There are guys who I like to hang out with, but I like to be the girl who no one can get. I think that's always hotter anyway. It's more attractive to be the person everyone talks about.'

MILEY'S DATING ADVICE

For Miley, there's nothing more important than being your own person and not compromising yourself for anyone. But that's not to say you shouldn't have the confidence to put yourself out there. As she says:

'I think confidence is the coolest thing. There will be times when guys are into me and I think I'm great on my own – I don't want someone rocking the boat. I feel like I take care of myself and I don't need someone else messing things up. I guess if you find a guy that you like, then go for it.'

Miley can sometimes be a dare-devil in her hunt for love too. 'I've done some pretty crazy stuff,' admits Miley. 'The craziest was probably when I was at summer church camp. I saw this guy and I was like, "Oh my gosh, he's so cute!" He was doing back flips off the diving board and he said to me that I should try it. I was so nervous, but I just kept telling myself, "Just go, you can do it." So I did, and I did a double back flip! It didn't work out between us, but I proved to myself I could do the flip.'

Nick Jonas

On the face of it, Nick ticks all the boxes. He's trendy, good-looking and shares similar career interests with Miley. Like Miley, he works with his family every day so he also holds similar family values to her.

We already know that the star of the Jonas Brothers and Miley share a history from when they allegedly hooked up on the *Best of Both Worlds* tour, so there's certainly plenty of chemistry there. They know each other well from touring, but they could get on each other's nerves having already spent so much time together. Nick certainly appeals to the Hannah in Miley, as his pop-star persona has similar glitz and glamour appeal as Miley's alter ego. But where does the fantasy end and the reality begin? And is it all a bit 'been there, done that' for Miley?

DATEABILITY 7/10

Zac Efron

The gorgeous *High School Musical* hunk would certainly meet and exceed all of Miley's expectations in the looks department. Plus he comes from a very similar background, having made his career at Disney. The two share a love of music and acting, and they love to sing, dance and perform in front of large audiences. He is a few years older, but Miley is very mature for her age. Zac is one of the few youth stars who would be able to understand and sympathise with the intense media attention Miley receives. Plus they already know each other from Miley's cameo in *High School Musical 2* and various Disney promo gigs. So, all in all, they seem like the perfect couple on paper. One snag, however, is Vanessa Hudgens, who's not only Zac's girlfriend, but also Miley's BFF. Oh well, maybe in another lifetime!

DATEABILITY 5/10

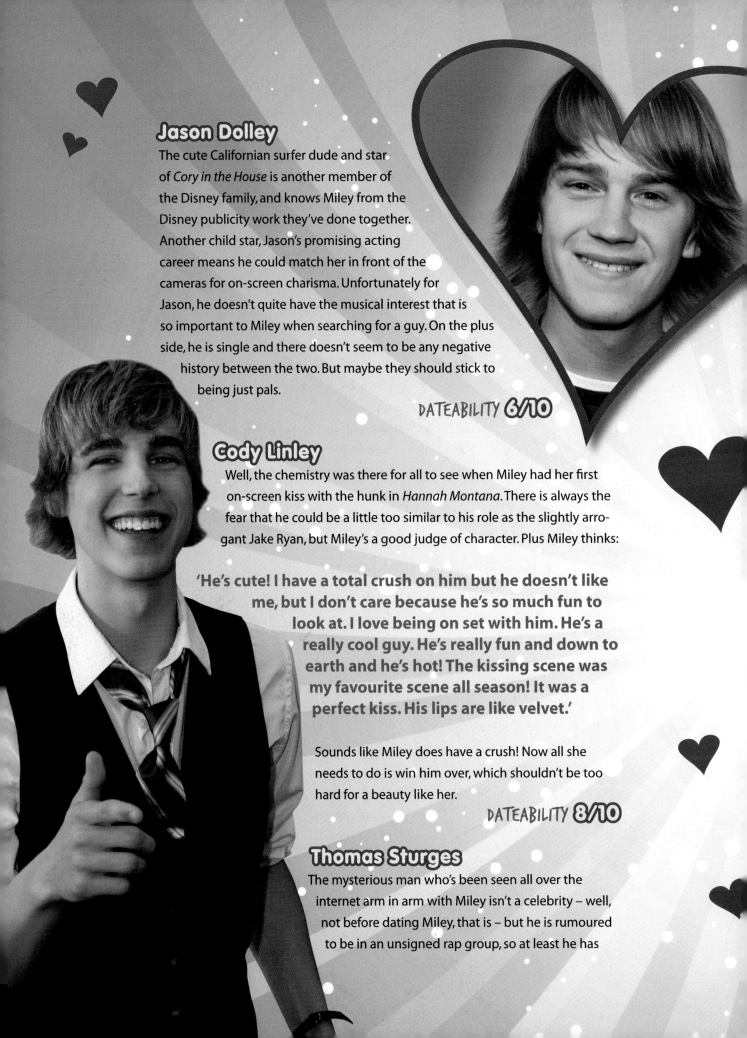

Jason Dolley

The cute Californian surfer dude and star of *Cory in the House* is another member of the Disney family, and knows Miley from the Disney publicity work they've done together. Another child star, Jason's promising acting career means he could match her in front of the cameras for on-screen charisma. Unfortunately for Jason, he doesn't quite have the musical interest that is so important to Miley when searching for a guy. On the plus side, he is single and there doesn't seem to be any negative history between the two. But maybe they should stick to being just pals.

DATEABILITY **6/10**

Cody Linley

Well, the chemistry was there for all to see when Miley had her first on-screen kiss with the hunk in *Hannah Montana*. There is always the fear that he could be a little too similar to his role as the slightly arrogant Jake Ryan, but Miley's a good judge of character. Plus Miley thinks:

'He's cute! I have a total crush on him but he doesn't like me, but I don't care because he's so much fun to look at. I love being on set with him. He's a really cool guy. He's really fun and down to earth and he's hot! The kissing scene was my favourite scene all season! It was a perfect kiss. His lips are like velvet.'

Sounds like Miley does have a crush! Now all she needs to do is win him over, which shouldn't be too hard for a beauty like her.

DATEABILITY **8/10**

Thomas Sturges

The mysterious man who's been seen all over the internet arm in arm with Miley isn't a celebrity – well, not before dating Miley, that is – but he is rumoured to be in an unsigned rap group, so at least he has

the musical talents Miley looks for in her boyfriends. Not much else is known about Thomas, but the fact that he's a normal guy, leading a normal life could appeal to the Miley Stewart in Miley. There's clearly an attraction between the two, but how much, only they know ...

DATEABILITY 8/10

Miley's favourite novel is *Don't Die, My Love* by Lurlene McDaniel.

Jesse McCartney

This gorgeous star seems to be a perfect match for Miley. He's super-successful on the music scene, having been a huge hit with his band, Dream Team, and most recently a smash-hit solo artist. And just like Miley, he acts as well as sings. Plus we know Miley has a crush on him from the *Hannah Montana* episode in which he was Hannah's dream boyfriend. But he is five years older than her, so the age gap could be a bit of a problem. Maybe in a few years, Miley.

DATEABILITY 6/10

Mitchel Musso

Well, they have a professional interest in each other and are both from southern US, which is important to Miley: 'I'm from the American South and down there we're all about southern hospitality.'

It's obvious that Mitchel and Miley share a close bond, but more than anything it's friendship rather than romance. But friendship can often turn into the best kind of love. For now, they're just great pals. According to Mitchel: 'Miley's been my best friend for like two years, so it's really easy going to work every day with your best friend.'

DATEABILITY 6/10

Miley and Her Pals

Girlfriends are much more important to Miley than boys, especially if she's having boy trouble: 'When I was going through a hard time about a boy, my friend spent the night talking to me. She let me talk all night. I just sat there, like, "I miss him".'

'Girlfriends are so important, as there is no time for dating right now,' says Miley. 'I'm too busy working to have a boyfriend – I think my dad likes this job because it keeps the boys away.'

MILEY'S SLEEPOVERS

Because she's on set all day, Miley's best time for hanging out with her friends is in the evening, and she just loves having her BFFs round to her house for sleepovers. 'I love sleepovers and just hanging out with my friends. I also love eating and watching TV or movies. Me and my friend bought twenty movies the other night and then watched all of them all day. We woke up at ten in the morning and watched them until eight p.m. We just got up every couple of hours for a coffee or something, and then came back to watch another one.'

'Because I work so much, mostly we just do sleepovers and hang out and play guitar. I'm teaching all my friends to play different instruments and music, and they tell me what's going on with their friends,' says Miley. 'I don't go to school with them, but I can hear about all the things that are going on at their high school and what's normal.'

As well as her normal friends, Miley loves to hang out with fellow superstars just like her two TV personalities, Miley Stewart and Hannah:

'I'm super lucky to live near my close friends Ashley Tisdale and Vanessa Hudgens. Vanessa and I were sleeping over at Ashley's one night. V and I shared one bed and Ash slept in the other.'

No doubt they stayed up all night gossiping about Zac and the Jonas brothers!

Miley became good friends with her Hannah Montana co-stars Emily Osment (Lilly) and Mitchel Musso (Oliver) when they met on set. They text each other when they're on stage and they use three-way calling to talk when they are at home.

Which Hannah Montana Star Are You?

1 **You're out to the movies on a hot date. Which film would you most like to see?**
- a) *The Alamo*
- b) *Chicago*
- c) *The Matrix*
- d) *Moulin Rouge*
- ✓ e) *Wedding Crashers*
- f) *Elizabethtown*

2 **After the movie you go for a bite to eat. What would be your meal of choice?**
- a) Ribs and wings
- ✓ b) Chinese
- c) Anything with ice cream
- d) Mexican
- e) Pizza
- f) Sushi

3 **Which of the following artists gets the most airtime on your iPod?**
- a) Johnny Cash
- b) The Beatles
- c) Fall Out Boy
- d) Coldplay
- e) Blink 182
- ✓ f) Hilary Duff

5 *Which of the following stars is your greatest celebrity idol?*
- a) John Wayne
- b) Audrey Hepburn
- c) Keanu Reeves
- d) Richard Branagh
- e) Leonardo DiCaprio
- f) Dolly Parton ✓

4 *The weekend comes and you feel like hitting the outdoors. What's your idea of fun?*
- a) Strumming a guitar on the porch ✓
- b) A few holes of golf
- c) Skateboarding
- d) Outdoors? No thanks!
- e) Surfing or anything beachy
- f) Horse riding

6 *What do you think the key to stardom is?*
- a) Fate
- b) Talent and good looks
- c) Self-belief and a bit of luck
- d) Standing out from the crowd
- e) Hard work, dedication and a cool hairstyle
- f) Destiny and hard work ✓

(cont.)

7 *Which motto best suits your attitude towards school?*

a) It's ok to be different. Don't let anyone hold you back and go for what you want 110%

b) Keep your head down, do all your homework and never misbehave

c) Stay true to yourself. Don't follow the crowd

d) Form a good relationship with your teachers in order to get the best possible advantage from class

e) Do what's necessary in class to allow you to follow your extra-curricular dreams, like surfing and acting

f) Hard work is the key and always pays off in the end

8 *After school do you …*

a) Run straight home to practise your guitar and write some heartfelt lyrics

b) Go shopping

c) Shoot some hoops

d) Head to drama class then home to annoy your brothers and sisters

e) Hit the beach for some surfing then to the mall to buy the latest trendy threads

f) Go straight to singing practice before calling your best friend for a gossip

9 *What do you look for in a potential boyfriend/girlfriend?*
- a) Blonde hair and an elegant figure
- b) Honesty and good hair
- c) Good singing voice and celebrity status
- d) Fun sense of humour and awesome dance moves
- ✓ e) Someone who laughs a lot and makes you smile
- f) Good looks, genuine personality and an independent nature

10 *What's your guilty pleasure?*
- ✓ a) Singing in the shower
- b) Accessory shopping
- c) Cheese
- d) Watching endless musicals
- e) Dyeing your hair blonde
- f) Wearing wigs

So how did you get on? Find out by counting up which letter you answered the most.

If you scored mostly …

A's You've got all the roguish, fatherly charm of Billy Ray Cyrus

B's You've got the beauty and loyalty of Emily Osment

C's You've got all the honesty and silliness of Mitchell Musso

D's You've got the whacky humour of Jason Earles

E's You possess the gorgeous brilliance of Cody Linley

F's You've all the beauty, wit and humility of Miley Ray Cyrus

DRESS YOUR OWN
Miley and Hannah

Whether she's Miley or Hannah, this superstar is always dressed to impress, but do you think you could do a better job than the most elegant girl in Hollywood? Why not dress your own Miley and Hannah and see.

Fancy Miley

If she's got a hot date to the school dance, Miley likes to wear an elegant red or black dress with matching shoes. Simple, but still stunning!

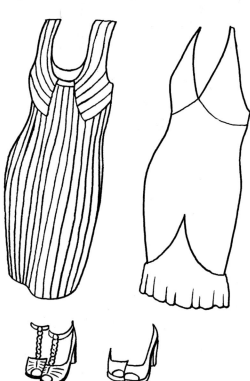

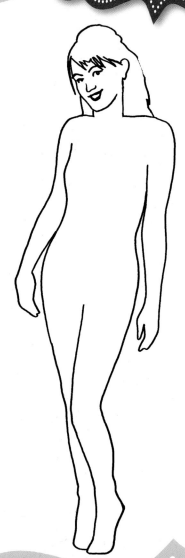

Chill-Out Miley

Around the house, Miley loves to keep it simple wearing casual jeans, a comfy T-shirt and a baby-blue jumper.

Instructions:

Cut out lots of different clothes from the pieces of paper (e.g. sparkly tops, comfy jeans, cool leggings, funky T-shirts, cosy jumpers, glamorous dresses and glittery scarves) and colour them in according to which style you chose. Using your glue, stick them to the different Miley and Hannah mannequins.

Out-and-about Hannah

When hanging out in LA, Hannah will try and stay incognito with a pair of gold sunglasses, a simple purple or white blazer, a funky pink T-shirt and grey or blue jeans. Don't forget her signature sparkly gold scarf!

Rock-out Hannah

When rocking the show, Hannah's favourite outfit is a pair of white jeans, a sparkly gold top and a red blazer. How cool!

Miley almost always wears a ring with the word 'Love' inscribed on it. It was a gift from her father to her mother, Tish.

SUDOKU

Fill in the boxes so that each one contains a drawing of the Hannah Montana gang – Hannah, Miley, Robbie Ray and Lilly. Don't forget, every row across and column down must contain all four pictures, so use a pencil before using a pen just in case you make a mistake!

	Hannah		Miley
Lilly	Robbie Ray	Miley	Hannah
Hannah		Robbie Ray	Lilly
Miley	Lilly		Robbie Ray

FORTUNE TELLER

Make your very own fortune teller to find out
what your and Miley's destiny holds.

You will need:
A square piece of paper
Pens
Pencils

Instructions:

1 Find the middle of the paper by folding it from corner to corner.

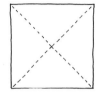

2 Fold each corner to the centre to make a smaller square.

3 Turn the square over, and turn each corner to the centre again to make an even smaller square.

4 Turn over again. Draw a different colour on each quarter of the square.

5 Turn over again. Put numbers 1 to 8 on each segment.

6 Open out each flap and write a message behind each number.

7 Put the thumb and forefinger of each hand into a segment and close up the fortune teller. First ask your pal to choose a colour. If they choose BLUE, spell out B-L-U-E and open and shut the fortune teller four times. Then ask your pal to choose a number from the four numbers showing. Open and shut the fortune teller the same number of times. Then, ask them to choose another number, open up the flap and read them the message hidden underneath.

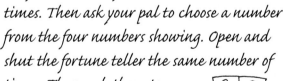

Fill your Miley fortunes with great predictions like ...

ROCK OUT WITH HANNAH TONIGHT
HANNAH AND JAKE FOREVER
YOU'RE MILEY'S BFF
MILEY IS, LIKE, SO OVER YOU

Rising star

MONTANA MOVIE MANIA

The year 2009 promises to be huge for both Miley and Hannah, with a third season of the hit TV show in the pipeline, so there are plenty of exciting times ahead. But the biggest event in 2009 is surely going to be the release of *Hannah Montana: The Movie*. Everyone is keeping fairly quiet about what we can expect from the film, but we do know that Miley's dad, Billy Ray, is one of the producers, and that some of the film will be set in her home state, Tennessee. So, perhaps the film will be a homecoming of sorts?

Some of the stars expected to be starring in it are old Hannah Montana faves Dolly Parton and Dwayne 'The Rock' Johnson. Plus there are murmurs of an appearance from Heather Locklear and Billy Ray's old hero, Willie Nelson. It's due to come out next May ... can't wait!

MUSIC OR MOVIES?

Miley's so talented that she's already a star of the music and television industry, and soon she's going to be bigger than ever when she hits the big screen with *Hannah Montana: The Movie*, but she says that her major goal for the moment is becoming a recognised musician:

'I can't wait to be known as Miley Cyrus the singer. Disney thought it would be great if not only Hannah Montana was a singer, but Miley was as well. They've been talking about Hannah Montana opening for Miley Cyrus and for us to do concerts together.'

Wow, that'll be one great show.

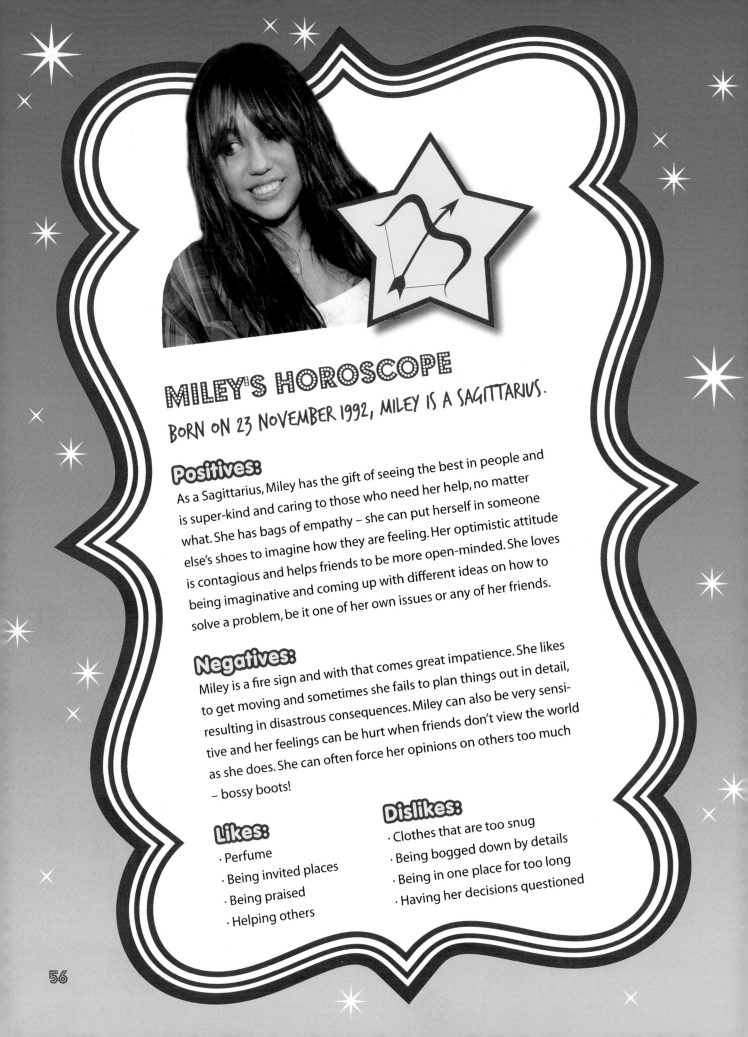

MILEY'S HOROSCOPE

BORN ON 23 NOVEMBER 1992, MILEY IS A SAGITTARIUS.

Positives:

As a Sagittarius, Miley has the gift of seeing the best in people and is super-kind and caring to those who need her help, no matter what. She has bags of empathy – she can put herself in someone else's shoes to imagine how they are feeling. Her optimistic attitude is contagious and helps friends to be more open-minded. She loves being imaginative and coming up with different ideas on how to solve a problem, be it one of her own issues or any of her friends.

Negatives:

Miley is a fire sign and with that comes great impatience. She likes to get moving and sometimes she fails to plan things out in detail, resulting in disastrous consequences. Miley can also be very sensitive and her feelings can be hurt when friends don't view the world as she does. She can often force her opinions on others too much – bossy boots!

Likes:

· Perfume
· Being invited places
· Being praised
· Helping others

Dislikes:

· Clothes that are too snug
· Being bogged down by details
· Being in one place for too long
· Having her decisions questioned

ZODIAC COMPATIBILITY

Nick Jonas (Virgo)

If these two can strike a balance between Virgo Nick's need for security and Sagittarian Miley's need for adventure, they could be a fab couple. Sagittarians are the wild explorers and Virgos are the sensible ones with the map; Nick's ability to analyse problems will help to prevent Miley from going off in the wrong direction. As long as Sagittarian Miley can keep her temper under control and Virgo Nick can avoid being too critical, they could make a wonderful couple.

Jesse McCartney (Aries)

Two fire signs collide to make a great match! Jesse and Miley have a lot in common because they both love new adventures and neither one buys the whole fame thing, so that would never become an issue. Miley likes to make plans but if something doesn't work out, Jesse, ever the original one, will always come up with a new way to do it. Aries and Sagittarians may argue a bit but it's always resolved quickly, and no one gets hurt. Don't be surprised if you find these two on a camping trip.

Cody Linley (Scorpio)

While only three days separate their birthdays, there's a big difference in their star signs. Miley finds strange things fascinating and Scorpio Cody can be off-the-wall and whacky. Scorpios are control freaks, but good luck trying to control firey Miley! Both of them have very strong opinions and if they start arguing, Scorpios can be aloof, while Sagittarians can be blunt. On the positive side, they both love exploring new things or unravelling mysteries, so if they can find a way to work together, they might be able to overlook the things that would drive other people crazy.

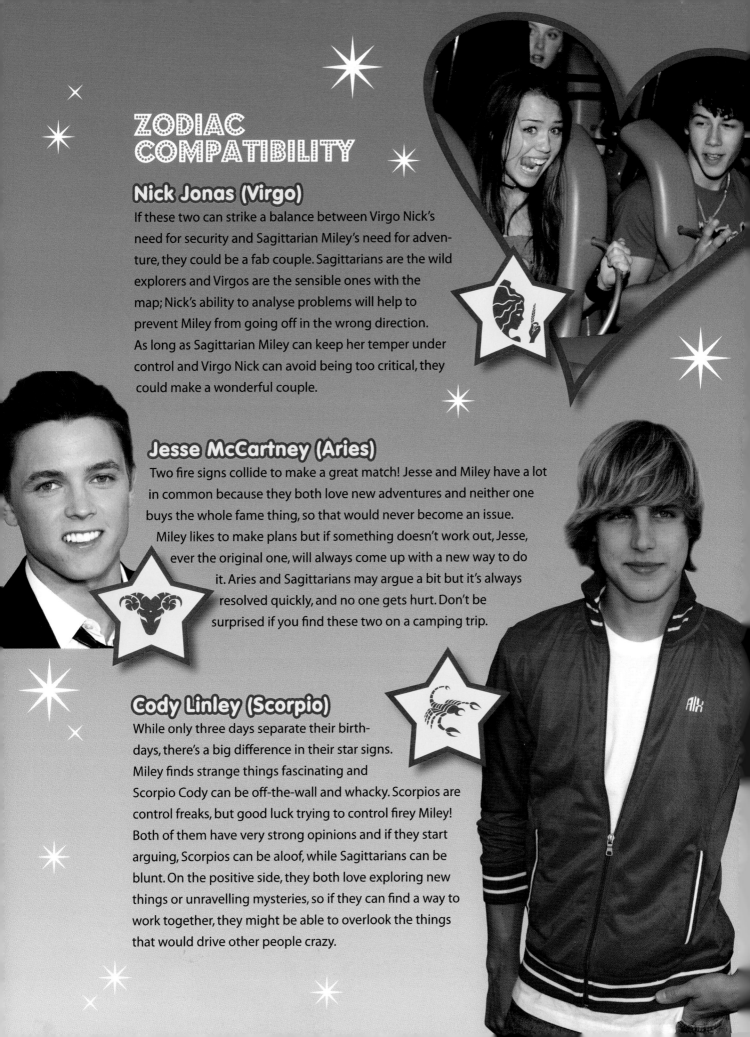

MILEY'S
2009 HOROSCOPE

Friends

This Sagittarian's got confidence galore this year. It's no wonder Miley's name is on all of the party invitation lists! She's going to have a blast in 2009.

Career

Things are going to get bigger and better for Miley in 2009. Big events are to come for her career around the middle of the year – perhaps a certain movie premiere?

Love

At the start of the year Miley will think she's ready to get more serious with her crush but then she'll have second thoughts. It's probably her inner voice giving her some good advice, so she should listen closely. Don't worry – things have a way of working out. In the meantime, she should relax and take things at her own pace.

So 2009 is looking bright for Miley Ray Cyrus. But what will happen in 2010 and beyond? WATCH THIS SPACE TO FIND OUT ...

ANSWERS

page 10: Miley Quiz

1. d) Destiny Hope Cyrus
2. a) Sagittarius
3. b) Nashville
4. d) Orlando Bloom
5. d) Hilary Duff
6. b) Smiley
7. d) Dog

8. b) *Steel Magnolias*
9. b) Roald Dahl
10. a) Spiders
11. b) Hot dogs
12. d) *Summerland*
13. a) Biting her nails
14. c) *Achy Breaky Heart*

15. b) Jennifer Aniston
16. d) Noah Lindsey
17. b) Vanilla
18. a) Chad Michael Murray
19. a) Elvis
20. c) Dolly Parton

page 29: Wordsearch

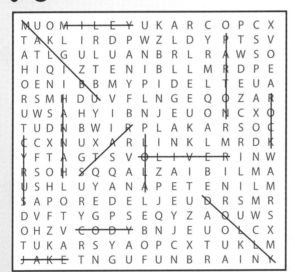

```
M U O M I L E Y U K A R C O P C X
T A K L I R D P W Z L D Y P T S V
A T L G U L A N B R L R A W S O
H I Q I Z T E N I B L L M R D P E
O E N I B B M Y P I D E L T E U A
R S M H D U V F L N G E Q O Z A R
U W S A H Y I B N J E U O N C X O
T U D N B W I R P L A K A R S O C
C C X N U X A R L I N K L M R D K
Y F T A G T S V O L I V E R I N W
R S O H S Q Q A L Z A I B I L M A
U S H L U Y A N A P E T E N I L M
S A P O R E D E L J E U D R S M R
D V F T Y G P S E Q Y Z A Q U W S
O H Z V C O D Y B N J E U O L C X
T U K A R S Y A O P C X T U K L M
J A K E T N G U F U N B R A I N Y
```

page 52: Sudoku

1st line: Robbie Ray, Hannah, Lilly, Miley
2nd line: Lilly, Robbie Ray, Miley, Hannah
3rd line: Hannah, Miley, Robbie Ray, Lilly
4th line: Miley, Lilly, Hannah, Robbie Ray

PICTURE CREDITS

First published in hardback in Great Britain in 2008 by
Orion Books
an imprint of the Orion Publishing Group Ltd
Orion House, 5 Upper St Martin's Lane,
London WC2H 9EA
An Hachette Livre UK Company

1 3 5 7 9 10 8 6 4 2

A CIP catalogue record for this book is available
from the British Library.

ISBN: 978 1 4091 0131 4

Designed by Goldust Design
Printed in Italy by Rotolito Lombarda

www.orionbooks.co.uk